Lights On! How Electricity Changed Our Lives

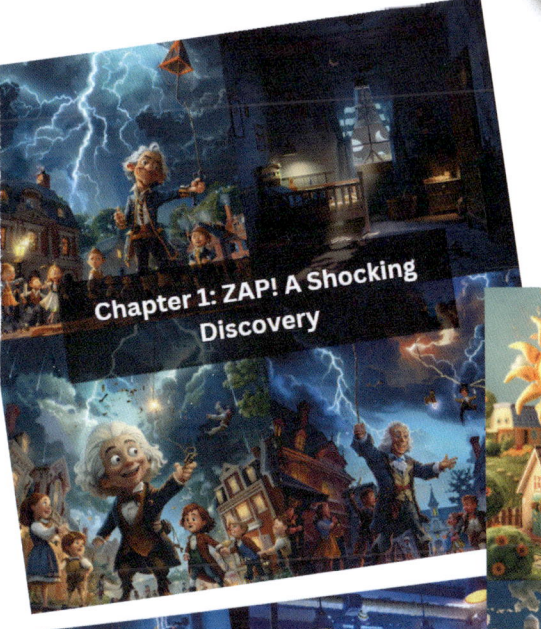

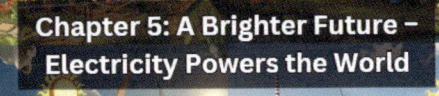

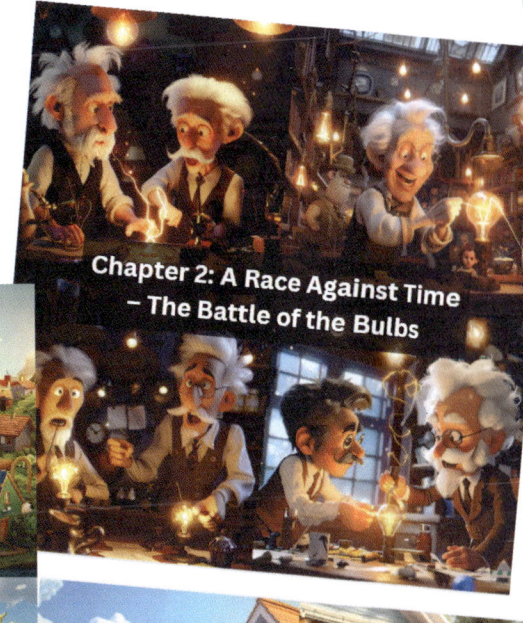

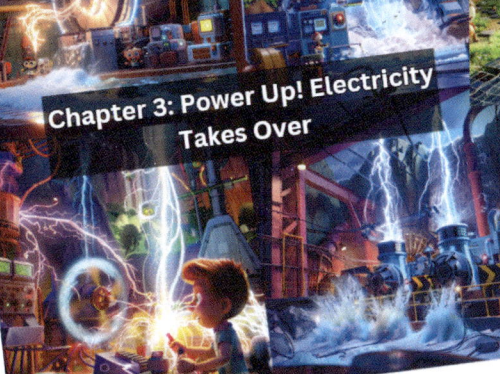

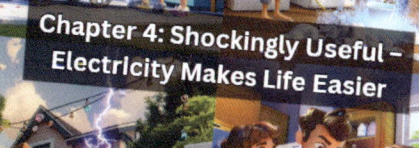

Chapter 1: ZAP! A Shocking Discovery

Chapter 2: A Race Against Time – The Battle of the Bulbs

Chapter 3: Power Up! Electricity Takes Over

Chapter 4: Shockingly Useful – Electricity Makes Life Easier

Chapter 5: A Brighter Future – Electricity Powers the World

Chapter 1: ZAP! A Shocking Discovery

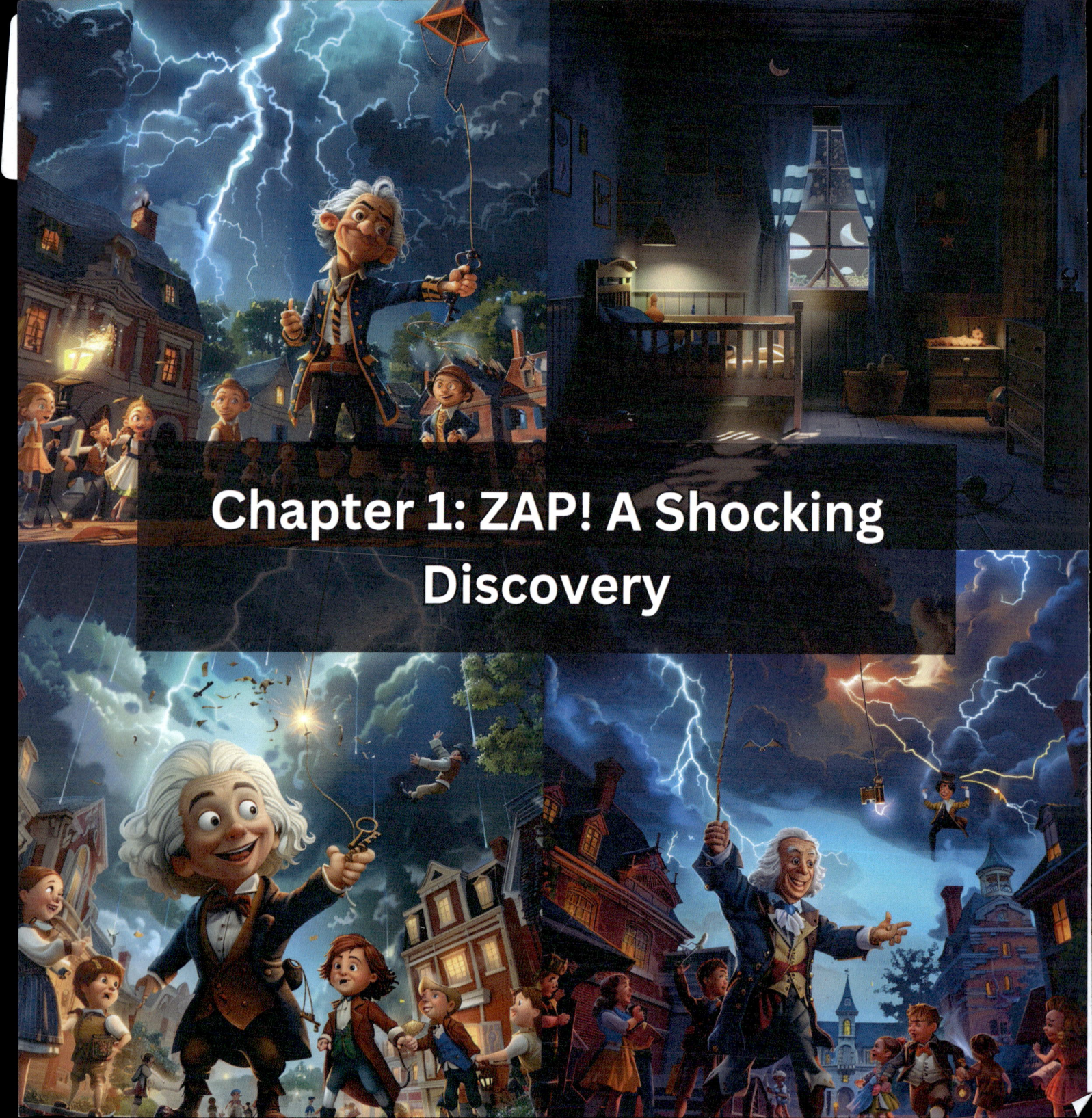

Imagine a world without light switches. No flicking on a lamp to chase away bedtime shadows.

No buzzing refrigerator keeping your lunch cool. This was life for kids like you way back when, all thanks to the absence of our amazing friend – electricity!

But how did this invisible force come to be? It all started with a curious fellow named Benjamin Franklin. Now, Ben wasn't afraid of a little storm.

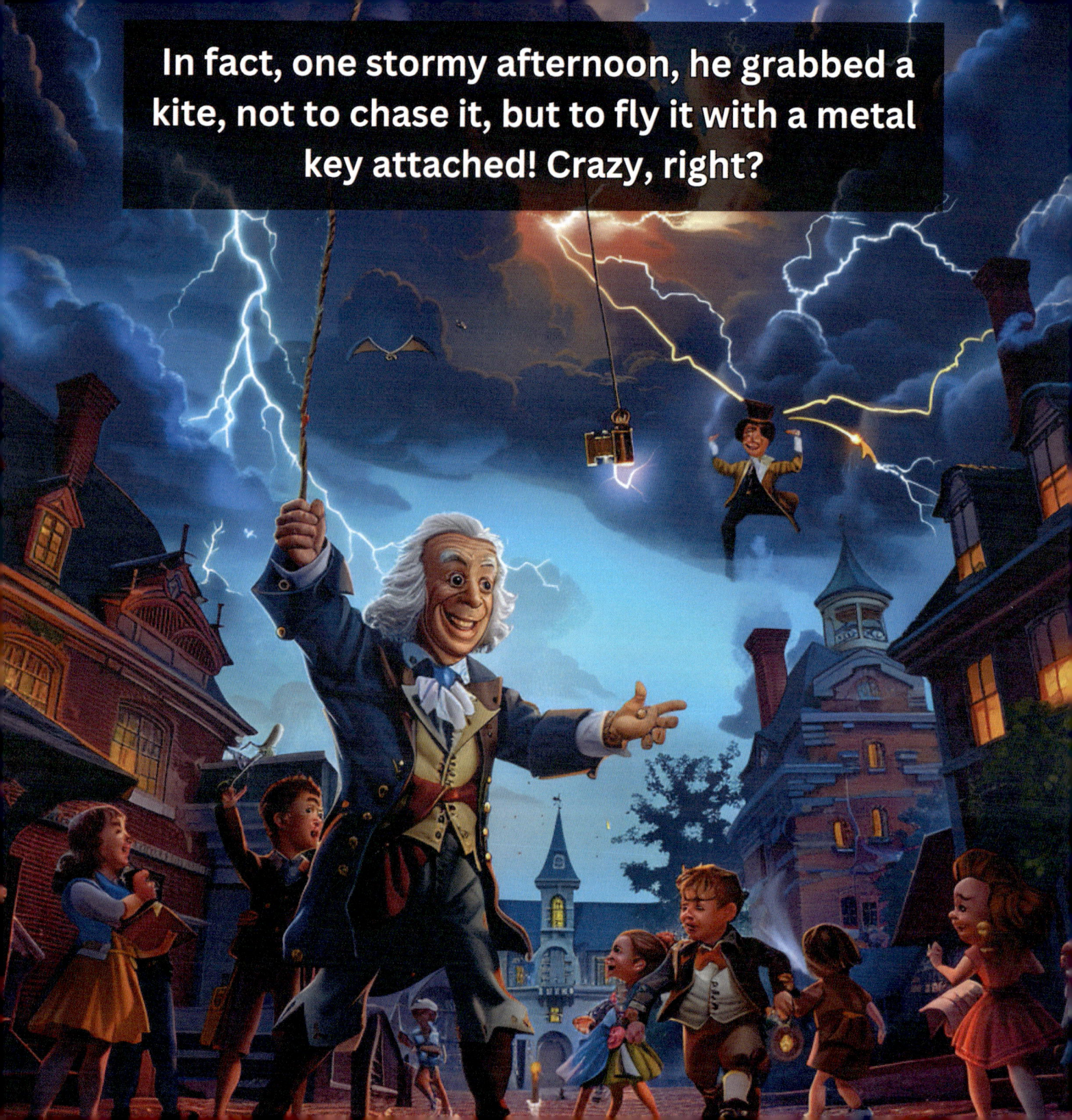

In fact, one stormy afternoon, he grabbed a kite, not to chase it, but to fly it with a metal key attached! Crazy, right?

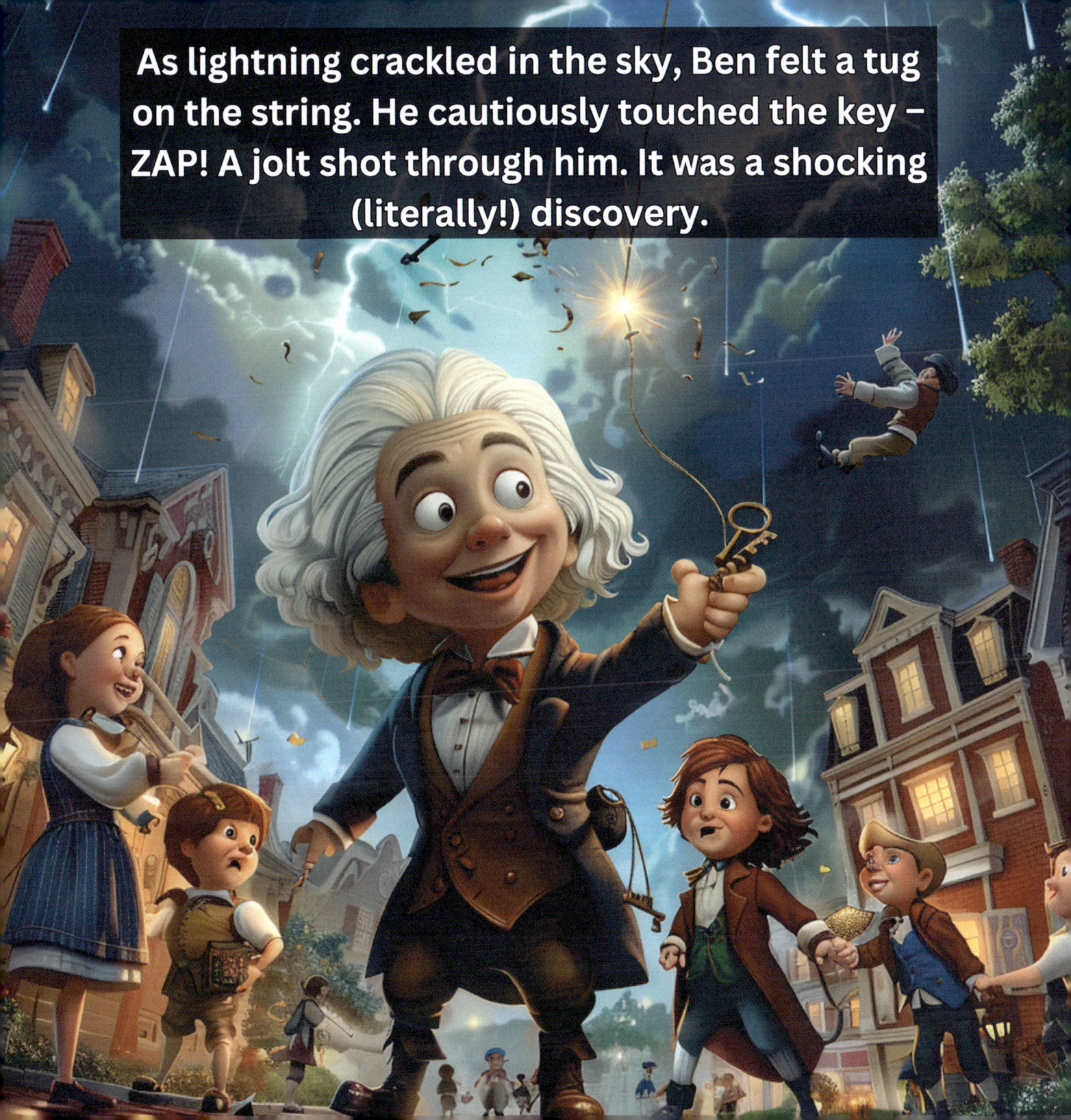

As lightning crackled in the sky, Ben felt a tug on the string. He cautiously touched the key – ZAP! A jolt shot through him. It was a shocking (literally!) discovery.

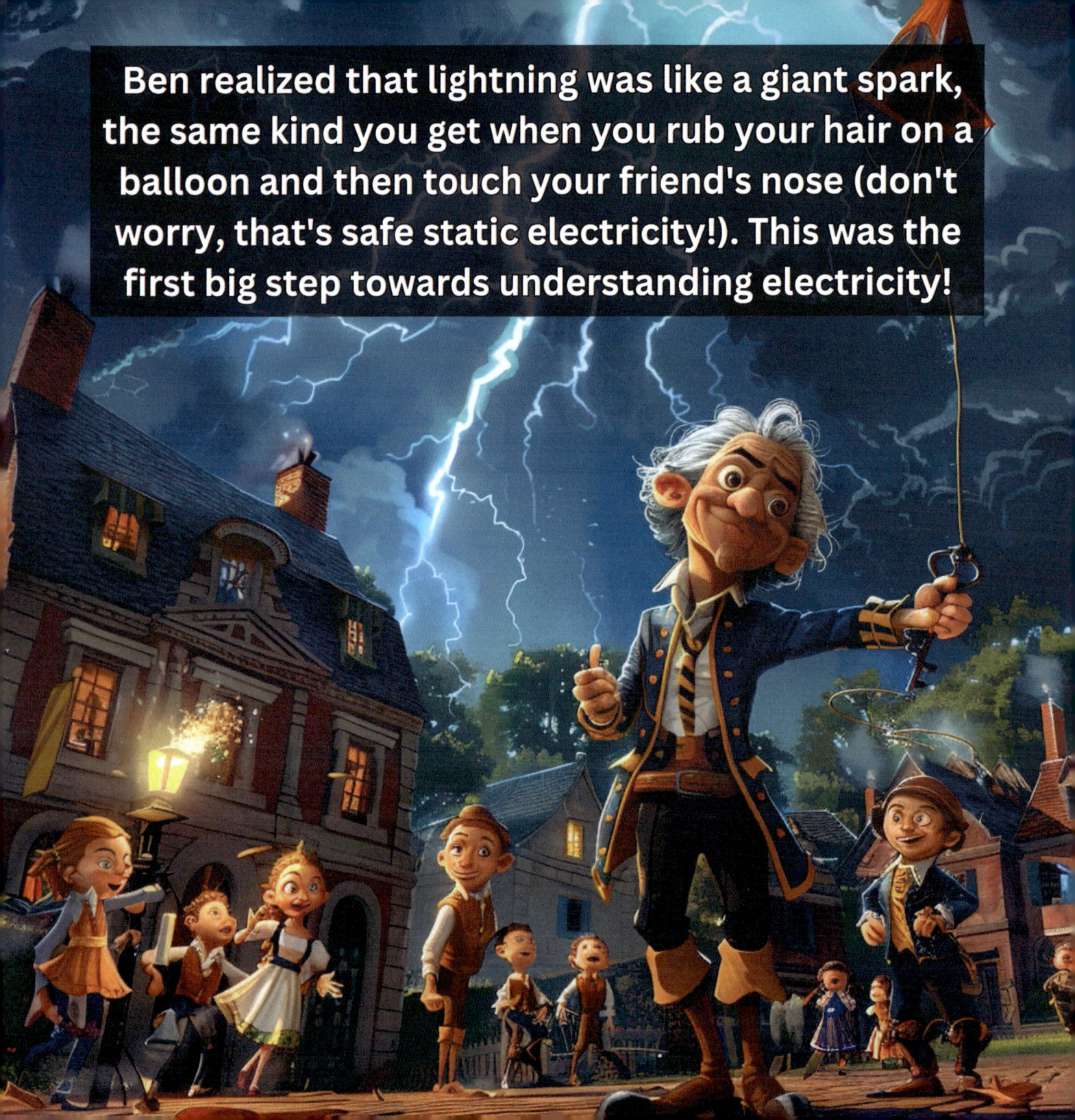

Ben realized that lightning was like a giant spark, the same kind you get when you rub your hair on a balloon and then touch your friend's nose (don't worry, that's safe static electricity!). This was the first big step towards understanding electricity!

Chapter 2: A Race Against Time – The Battle of the Bulbs

Fast forward a few centuries. People were tired of using flickering candles and smelly oil lamps. They wanted something brighter, something... electric!

Two inventors, Thomas Edison and Joseph Swan, were locked in a race to create the first long-lasting electric light bulb.

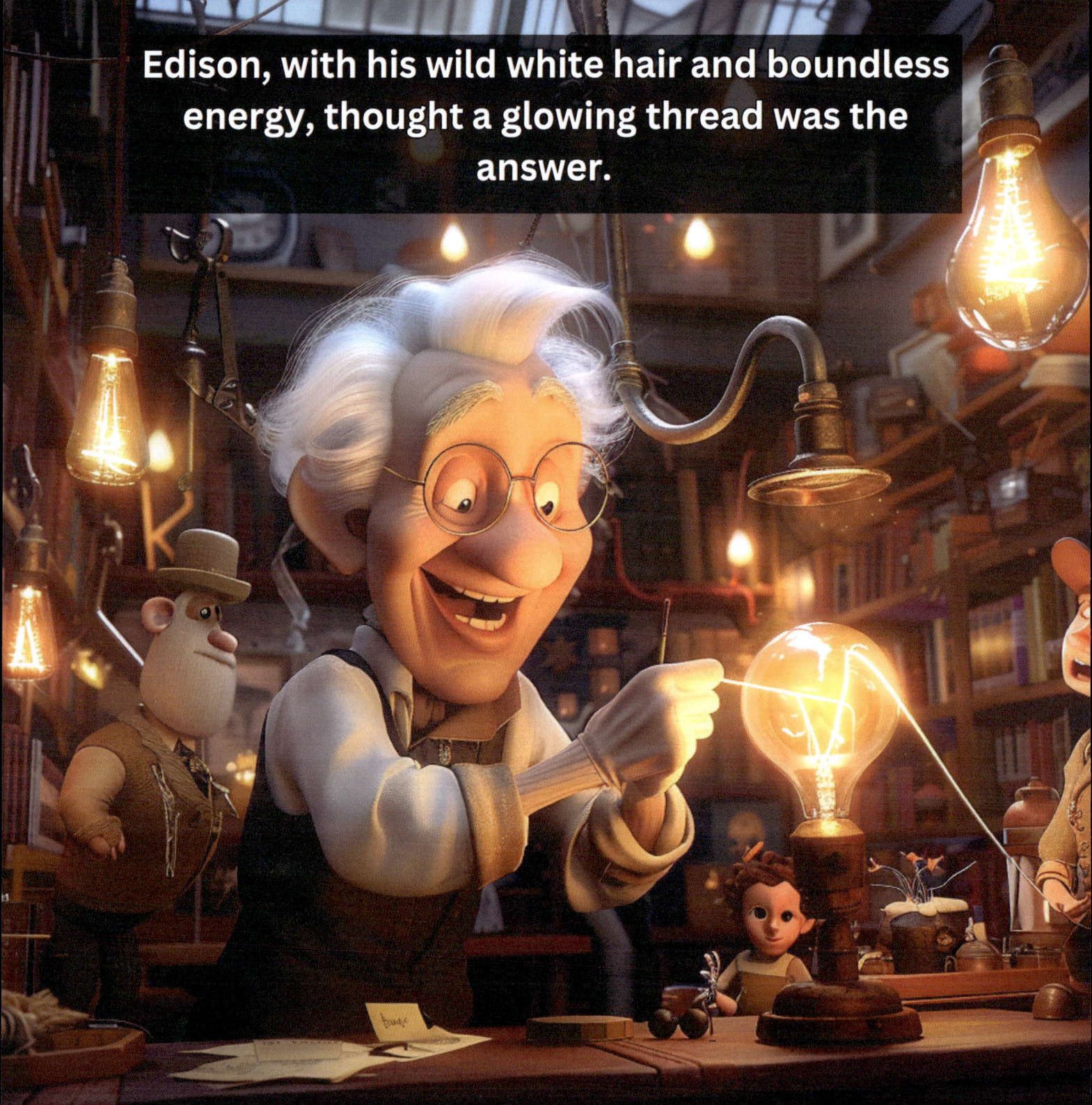

Edison, with his wild white hair and boundless energy, thought a glowing thread was the answer.

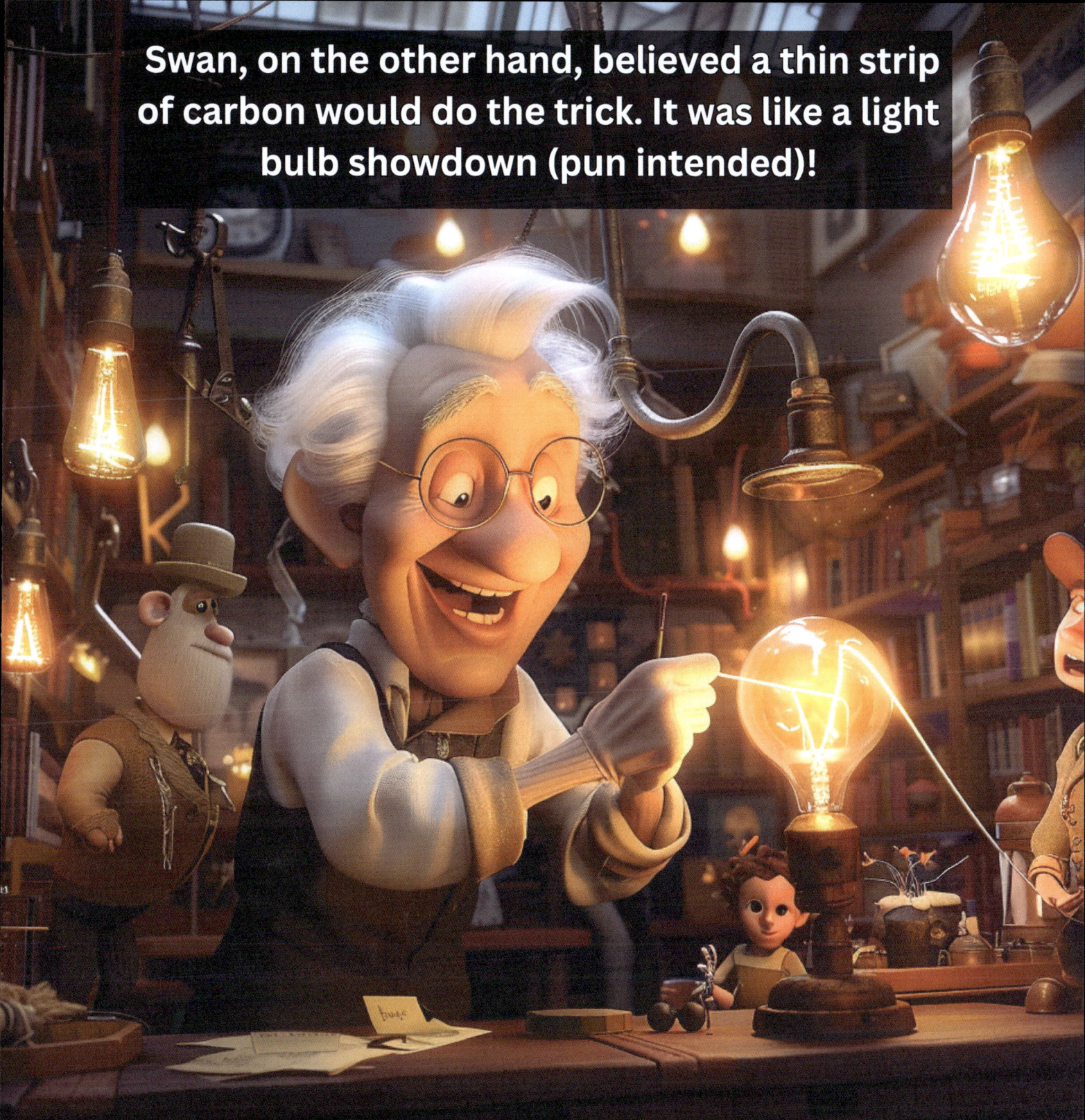

Swan, on the other hand, believed a thin strip of carbon would do the trick. It was like a light bulb showdown (pun intended)!

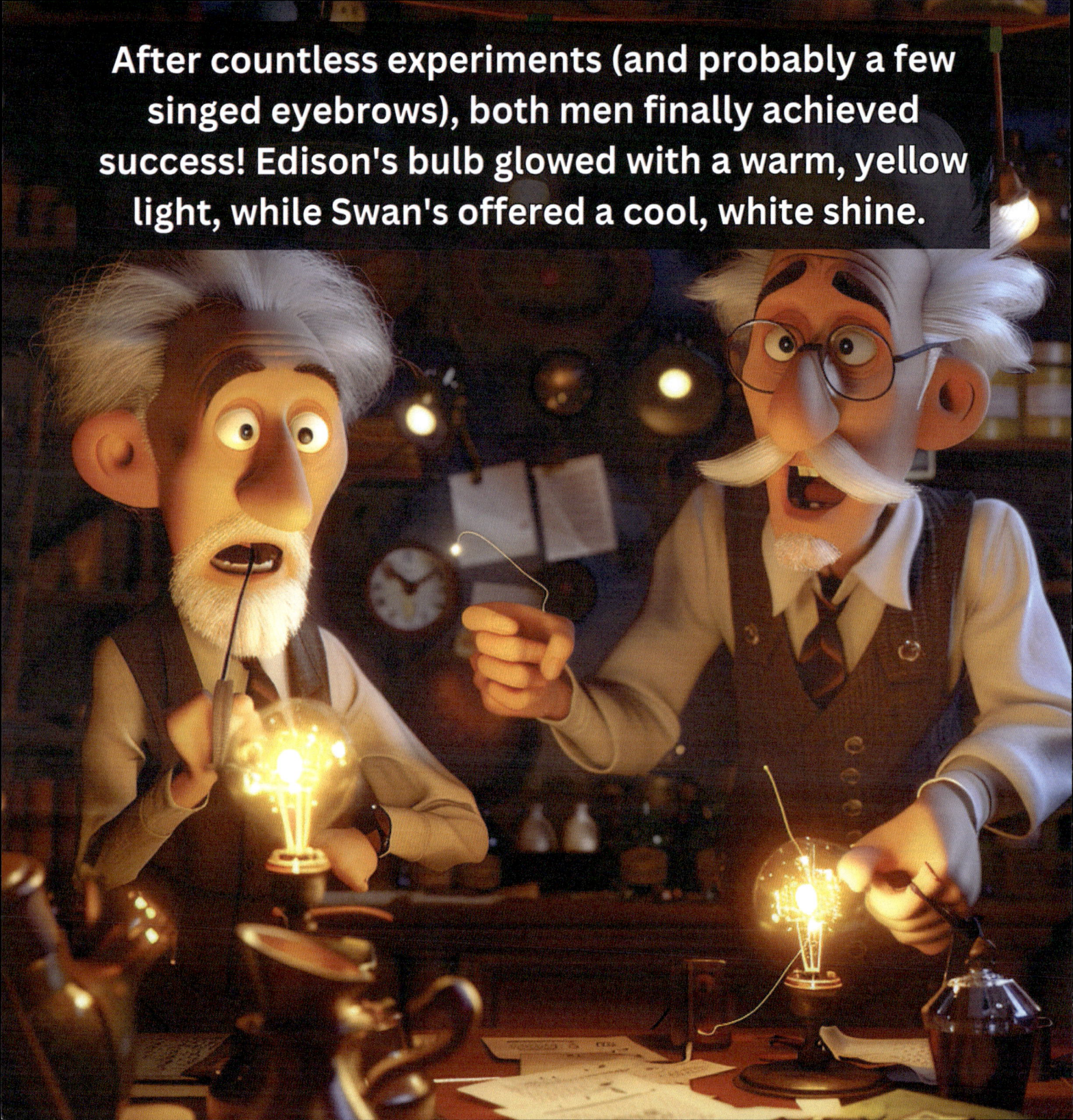

After countless experiments (and probably a few singed eyebrows), both men finally achieved success! Edison's bulb glowed with a warm, yellow light, while Swan's offered a cool, white shine.

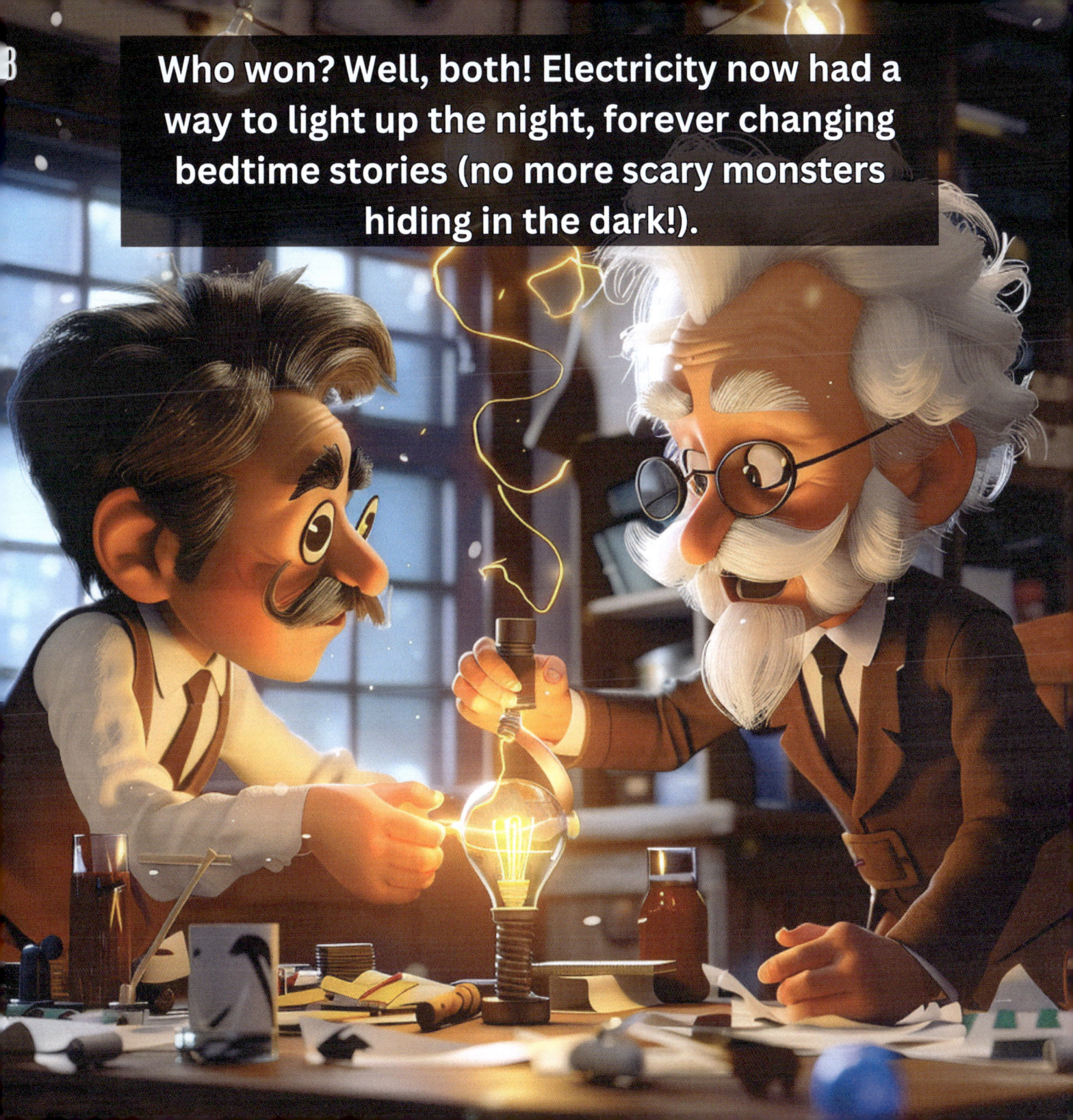

Who won? Well, both! Electricity now had a way to light up the night, forever changing bedtime stories (no more scary monsters hiding in the dark!).

Chapter 3: Power Up! Electricity Takes Over

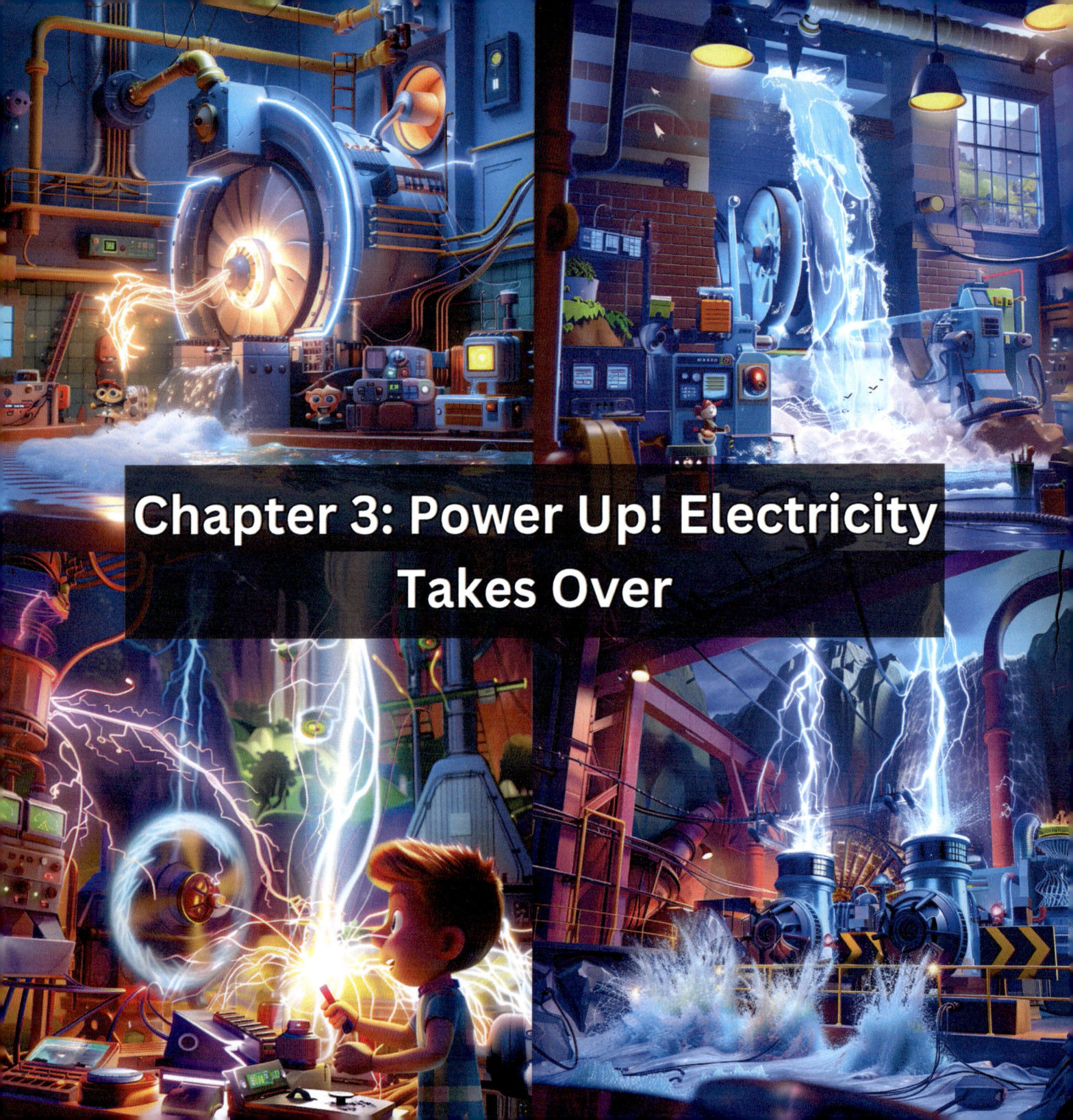

Think about all the amazing gadgets you use every day – your video game console, your music player, even your toaster! But before electricity, these were just dreams.

With the invention of power plants, electricity became like a tireless runner, zipping through wires and powering homes and businesses.

Imagine a giant spinning wheel (called a turbine) being pushed by rushing water or hot steam. This spinning creates a magical force – magnetism.

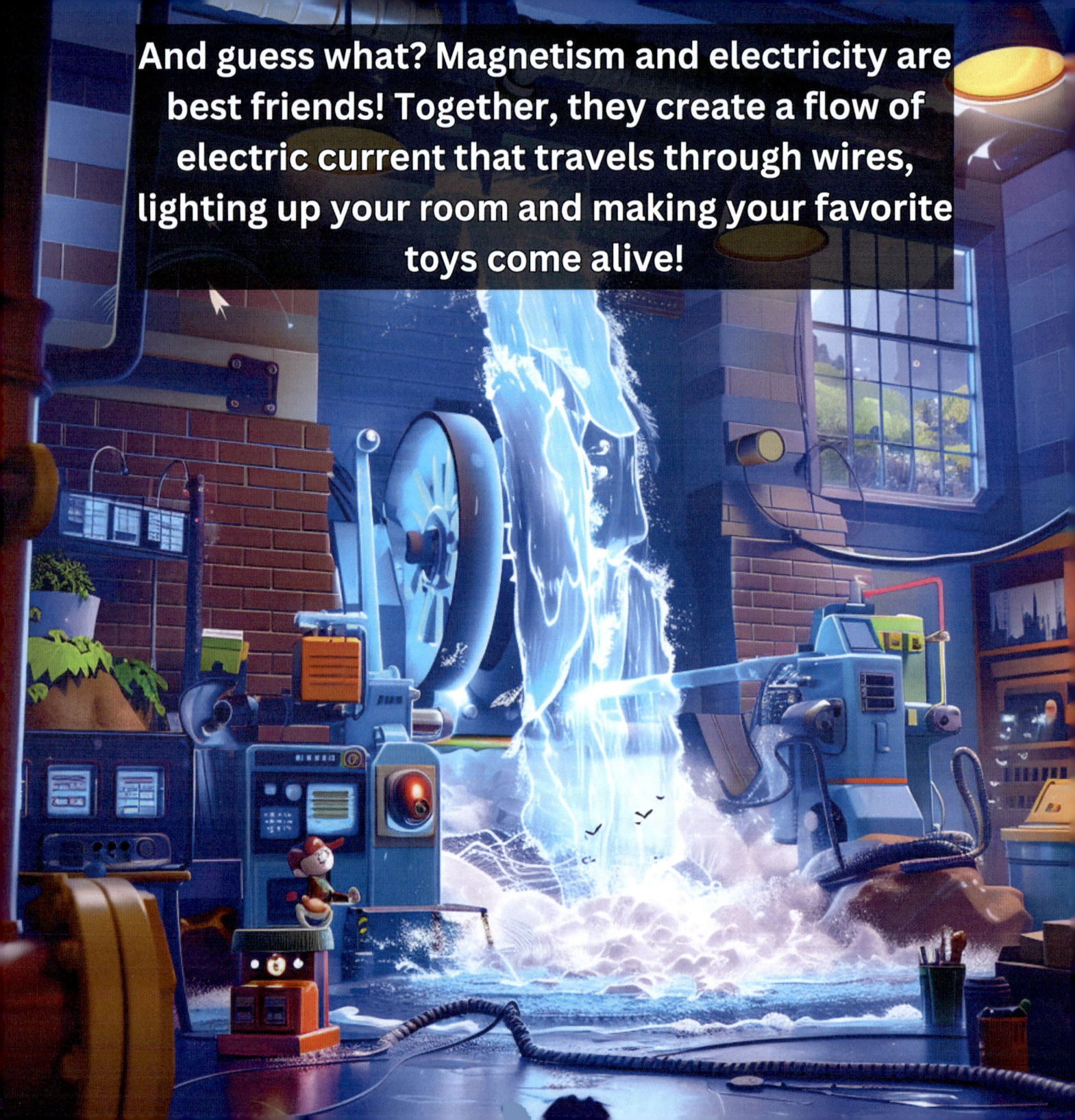

And guess what? Magnetism and electricity are best friends! Together, they create a flow of electric current that travels through wires, lighting up your room and making your favorite toys come alive!

Chapter 4: Shockingly Useful – Electricity Makes Life Easier

Electricity wasn't just for entertainment. It made life a whole lot easier! Remember those long summer days spent churning ice cream by hand?

Well, electric motors took over that job, giving you more time for fun in the sun (and delicious ice cream breaks!).

Electricity also helped keep food fresh with the invention of the refrigerator. No more daily trips to the market! And those long evenings spent scrubbing clothes by hand?

Washing machines became electric superheroes, saving your arms (and probably your patience) from endless scrubbing.

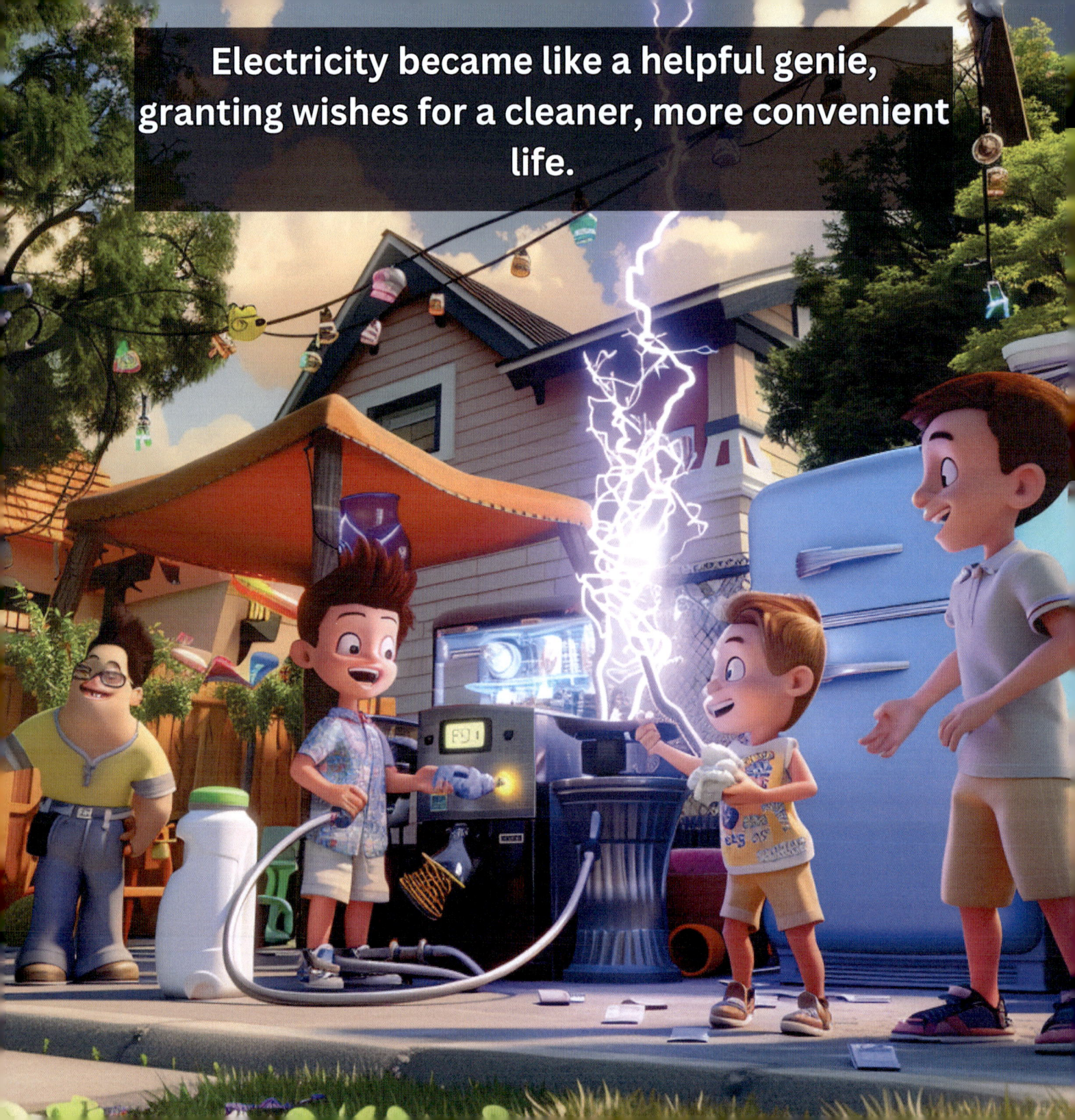

Electricity became like a helpful genie, granting wishes for a cleaner, more convenient life.

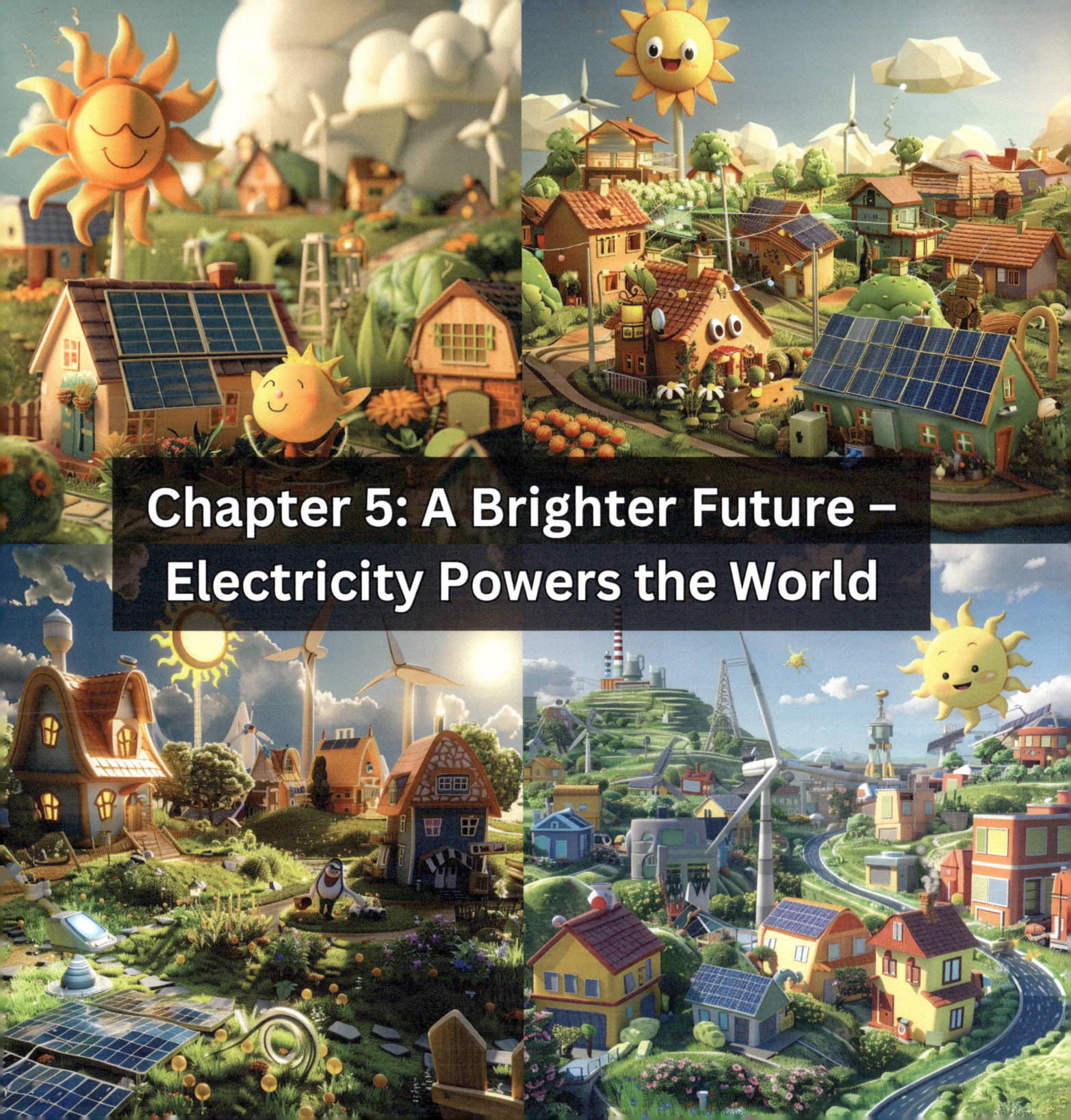

Chapter 5: A Brighter Future – Electricity Powers the World

Today, scientists are constantly finding new ways to use electricity. Solar panels capture the sun's energy, windmills use the power of wind, and even water rushing down rivers can be used to generate electricity! This is called renewable energy, and it's helping us take care of our planet for future generations.

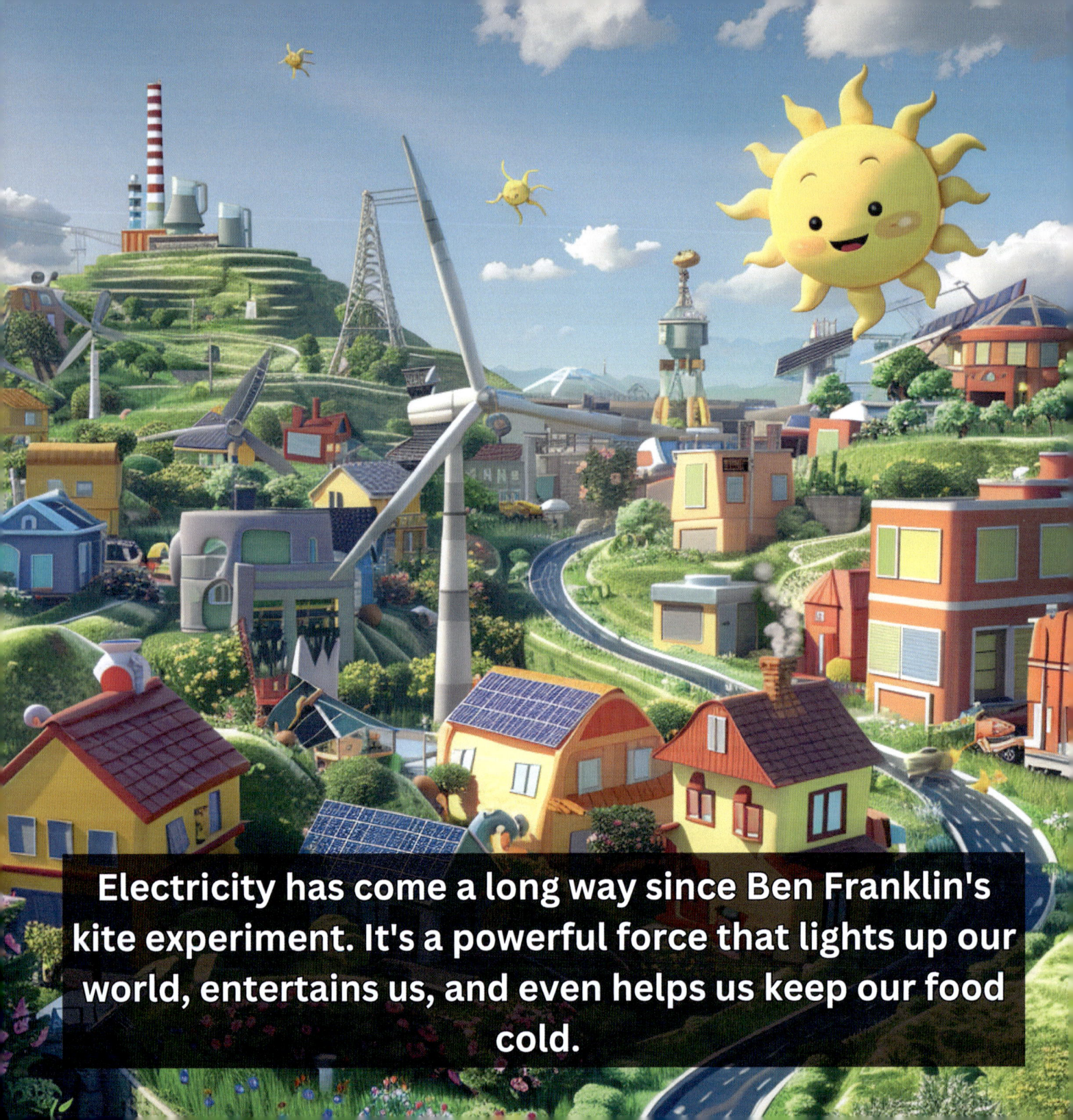

Electricity has come a long way since Ben Franklin's kite experiment. It's a powerful force that lights up our world, entertains us, and even helps us keep our food cold.

So next time you flip on a light switch, take a moment to appreciate the amazing journey of electricity and how it changed our lives forever!

Printed in Great Britain
by Amazon